SUMMERTREE

Ron Cowen

SUMMERTREE

Random House
New York

For *Jerome Lawrence*
Most people think playwriting
can't be taught.

A MONOLOGUE WITH THE AUTHOR

(Ron Cowen *doodles in ink on a large sheet of paper*)

Summertree is a play of commonplaces. An anti-war message. A young man in search of identity! A father in search of . . . his strength? Their clash!

(*A peevish grin*)

Labeled and categorized generation gap for easy handling.

(*More doodling*)

Someone dying saying, "Remember me." Characters and their problems, easily recognizable. Seen again. They have no names. You may name them yourselves.

(*To himself, concentrating hard to figure out what he wrote*)

Confrontations, but no climax. Action doesn't really build either inevitably or by accident to a climax. No special date or place. A common place, a tree.

(*He smiles*)

No hero! No tragic bout with fate! No tragic flaw! No circumstances that leave no way out! There are ways out.

(*A pause*)

Was the hero a great pianist!

(*More doodling*)

All the little problems, the little crises, the little misunderstandings, day to day. How important they must seem on the day you know it is the last day you'll have them. Saying *Summertree* over and over so fast that it starts sounding like cemetery. Everything, though commonplace, must be remembered.

(*Crumpling the doodles*)

What a waste, the plans and problems. The tragedy is only the tragedy of waste. Waste is very commonplace.

Fadeout

SUMMERTREE *was first produced in New York City on March 3, 1968, and presented by the Repertory Theater of Lincoln Center with the following cast:*

(*In order of appearance*)

YOUNG MAN	David Birney
LITTLE BOY	Barry Symonds (or Donnie Melvin)
MOTHER	Priscilla Pointer
FATHER	Philip Sterling
GIRL	Blythe Danner
SOLDIER	Tom Fuccello

Directed by David Pressman
Production Stage Manager Ronald Schaeffer
Stage Manager Seth Glassman
Electrician Lester Herzog
Properties Henry Dacyger
Production Secretary Janet Kelley

SUMMERTREE *was first presented in a staged reading at the Eugene O'Neill Memorial Theater Foundation Summer Playwrights, Conference in July, 1967, with the following cast:*

(*In order of appearance*)

YOUNG MAN	Michael Douglas
LITTLE BOY	Scott Jacoby
MOTHER	Rusti Moon
FATHER	Philip Sterling
GIRL	Jody Locker
SOLDIER	José Perez

Directed by Lloyd Richards

Act One

ACT ONE

The scene is a deep green glen. At the back is a large, gnarled, heavy trunk of a tree. It rises into branches which spread out. A couple of geraniums are planted at the base of the tree. The YOUNG MAN *is seated beneath the tree while the stage is dark.*

A machine-gun blast breaks the silence, followed quickly by a dim, broken, blue-light pattern on the stage floor. At this moment the GIRL *appears at stage right, carrying a portable tape recorder, which is playing a Bach fugue. She crosses the stage and exits, with the fugue still playing. As she crosses down stage center, the* SOLDIER *enters up stage left, runs to stage right, where he crouches a moment, then exits down stage right. As he crouches, the* BOY *enters and runs to the center of the stage; he looks right and left and then exits behind the tree. As he goes out, a red glow rises on the* YOUNG MAN. *The fugue slowly fades out during the first speech.*

YOUNG MAN   It's hot out here, just sitting and waiting. Shirt's sticking to my back. I hate it like this, wiping sweat out of my eyes. Damn. I'll just lie here and let the breeze cool my face. Ah. Just close my eyes and put my head back. I have to remember all these things. Hey, you're tickling me . . . ow! That hurts! Mom . . . Dad? . . . I wish you could feel the palm of my hand. Can you see how smooth it is? Can you tell that it is warm? There are all these lines. All these little lines going all over, criss-crossing, entwining, stop-

3

ping, then starting up again. (*He smiles and looks up*) You know, hands are like leaves. (*Embarrassed at being obvious*) But you know that. (*He picks up a leaf*) Ever peel a leaf? You know. You peel off the skin or the flesh . . . the green part . . . and try and just leave the veins without breaking any of them. (*Peeling the leaf*) Like this. (*To himself*) Very slowly. Very carefully. (*Holds up his partly peeled leaf*) You must do it very slowly and be very cautious not to break a vein in two. See? It looks like a winter tree. Then you hold it up to the sun and see how it makes a shadow. It looks like a big skeleton's hand. (*He smiles and looks up*) Did you ever wonder if a hand could be stripped like a leaf? (*He looks up*) It could, you know. Sure. You very slowly, very carefully, peel the skin away, being careful not to break anything. Then you hold the skeleton hand up to the light and see how it makes a shadow like a big winter tree. If you care to try it yourself, I guarantee you, you won't feel a thing. Except yourself . . . screaming. You know, this tree has been here for years and years. It's funny. The first thing I wanted to do when I was a kid was to dig it up and see it fall over. (*The* LITTLE BOY *enters*) I guess all kids do.

(*The lights rise on the* LITTLE BOY, *back under the tree. He is slamming the base of the tree with a hand hoe*)

LITTLE BOY (*Calling to the* YOUNG MAN) Hey, aren't you going to help me?

YOUNG MAN No.
(*He turns toward him and walks back. The lights rise*)

LITTLE BOY   Why not?

YOUNG MAN   Because it's a waste of time. You'll never dig up that tree.

LITTLE BOY   Yes I will.

YOUNG MAN   Look, do you know what roots are?

LITTLE BOY   Yes.

YOUNG MAN   What?

LITTLE BOY   They hold the tree in the ground.

YOUNG MAN   That's right. And do you know how big roots are?

LITTLE BOY   No. How big?

YOUNG MAN   Well, at least as big as the whole top part of the tree.

LITTLE BOY   How come?

YOUNG MAN   To keep the tree from falling over.

LITTLE BOY   How come people don't have roots?

YOUNG MAN   People do have roots. Except they're different. But they're still supposed to keep you from falling over.

5

LITTLE BOY   You're nuts.
(*He gives the* YOUNG MAN *a shove*)

YOUNG MAN   When I was your age we used to dig holes to the other side of the world.
(*The* YOUNG MAN *kneels beside him*)

LITTLE BOY   Why would you want to go there, anyhow?

YOUNG MAN   It's as good a place as any.

LITTLE BOY   Are you kidding? Don't you watch the news? There's a war over there.

YOUNG MAN   Everybody has wars.

LITTLE BOY   Why don't we just drop a great big bomb on them and blow them up? Boom.

YOUNG MAN   Because they'd drop one on us.

LITTLE BOY   Uh-uh. Because they'd all be dead.

YOUNG MAN   But what if they're not? You never know. Besides, you don't think it's right to kill people, do you?

LITTLE BOY   Only if they're bad.

YOUNG MAN   What do you mean, bad?

LITTLE BOY (*Jumps up, shouts impatiently*)   You kill them because they're your enemy!

6

YOUNG MAN   Do you mean that all those people over there that you don't even know are your enemy?

LITTLE BOY   Yes!

YOUNG MAN   Do you think they'd sneak in and kill you some night?

LITTLE BOY   I . . . don't know.

YOUNG MAN   Well, don't worry about it, they don't even know where you live.

LITTLE BOY   So what if they find out?

YOUNG MAN   Listen. Come here. They aren't going to kill you. I was only kidding you. Nobody wants to kill anybody.

LITTLE BOY   Then how come people do?
  (*He goes back to his digging*)

YOUNG MAN   Because . . . sometimes . . . when you don't understand something and you're afraid of it or something . . . maybe because it's bigger than you, or you think it's ugly . . . you think that unless you protect yourself from that thing, it will hurt you. And then maybe if it does something that scares you more . . . you either run away or try to protect yourself. And maybe kill it.

LITTLE BOY   So then it won't bother you any more.

7

YOUNG MAN But it's not that simple. What if the thing really wasn't doing anything to hurt you . . . you just thought it was?

LITTLE BOY Then you made a mistake. (*He shrugs*) What's it like to be dead?

YOUNG MAN I don't know. Why?

LITTLE BOY Just want to know.

YOUNG MAN I guess it's like nothing. You can't see anything or hear anything, and you can't feel anything or think about anything . . .

LITTLE BOY It sounds lonely.

YOUNG MAN Yes, I think so. (*He pauses*) But you've got a long time before you have to think about that. You've just started.
  (*Both exit*)

MOTHER (*Coming onstage*) He looks just like he did when he was a little boy. The other night I got out these old photographs—I haven't looked at them in years—and sorted through them, putting them in order. If there were a photograph for every day of his life, then I might feel he was almost nineteen. But a hundred or so photographs make nineteen years seem like a week and a half. It's not really fair. I found my two favorites . . . this one . . . (*She holds up a photograph*) When he was eight or nine. He's standing in front of our first television set in a cowboy suit.

He has on a ten-gallon hat and boots, and the loudest cap pistol on the block. The second photograph . . . (*She holds up a photograph*) is when he was just a baby—four or five. He's standing in his flannel pajamas, holding a giraffe we brought him back from Florida. It was yellow oilcloth with orange spots. He still has it. He says it's the oldest living possession he's got, and he's not giving it up. (*She smiles to herself*) It's much more difficult trying to give up people than it is giraffes. Especially sons. I'm not very good at it. It's lonely having him away at college. Even when he's home on vacation he doesn't like to stay around the house. (*The* YOUNG MAN *enters*) I wish I could find that drawing that he made of the tree. I can't remember what I did with it.

(*The lights begin to fade. The lights fade out on the* MOTHER *and rise on the* YOUNG MAN, *sitting on a stool, facing the tree. He has a sketch pad in his lap and some pastels. He is drawing the tree*)

FATHER (*Entering*)   How's it coming?

YOUNG MAN   I don't know. I don't feel anything.

FATHER   You're not concentrating. Where'd you get those?

YOUNG MAN   I bought them.

FATHER   With whose money?

YOUNG MAN   With my money—that I saved.

FATHER   All right. (*He pauses*) Have you thought about the fall?

YOUNG MAN   I told you. I'm not going back. I've had it.

FATHER   Just one lousy year to go, and you can't finish . . .

YOUNG MAN   I told you, I'll pay you back.

FATHER   The money isn't important.

YOUNG MAN   Since when isn't the money important?

FATHER (*Not hearing him*)   But to quit like that. What's one more year?

YOUNG MAN   I don't care.

FATHER   You don't care about anything. What do you care about?

YOUNG MAN   I don't know.

FATHER   Then if you're not going back to school, you should damned well get your ass in the army. They'll give you something to think about.

YOUNG MAN   That's your pat answer for everything, isn't it? Every time I say I don't care or I don't know, you say I should get my ass in the army.

FATHER   That's right.

YOUNG MAN   Well, I'm not.

FATHER   And since when do you get a choice?

YOUNG MAN   I said I'm not going. I'll go to prison.

FATHER   Yeah. I can just see you in prison, trying to call up for room service. Look, it's something you're going to have to do. That's all. Everybody does.

YOUNG MAN   No, that isn't all . . . and it isn't something everybody does.

FATHER   You could use the discipline. Learn how to take orders.

YOUNG MAN   I know how to take orders. But I'm not going to kill somebody because somebody tells me to. (*He pauses*) Could you kill someone?

FATHER   If I had to.

YOUNG MAN   If you had to . . . it's so easy for you to say that, but better me than you.

FATHER   That isn't true. I don't want you to kill and I don't want to see you . . . killed.

YOUNG MAN   Well, thank you. Your concern touches me.

FATHER   Go back to school. You still have your deferment.

YOUNG MAN   I will not go back unless I go to music school.

FATHER   Not on my money you won't.

YOUNG MAN   Then I'll have to work part time and go to school part time.

FATHER   You know as well as I do you'll get drafted doing that.

YOUNG MAN   All right. Forget it.
(*He takes the pastels and draws lines down his shirt*)

FATHER   What are you doing?

YOUNG MAN   You'll see.

FATHER   Stop it! Stop it!

YOUNG MAN   See? It's my coat of many colors. Just like Joseph. (*He takes off the shirt and hands it to the* FATHER. *The* FATHER *refuses to take it*) Have a robe?

FATHER   What's wrong with you?

YOUNG MAN (*Putting his shirt back on*)   I'm afraid of people like you, that's what's wrong with me. (*His voice trails off; then he shouts*) You're no help!
(*He exits*)

FATHER   No help . . . half the time I don't know what he's talking about. I don't do anything but help. Look at this shirt. Seven bucks for a shirt! (*Calling off to the* YOUNG

MAN) If I talked that way to my father—(*To the audience*) This idea of his, not going back to school, well, he's going back, I can tell you. I can afford to send him and he's going to get his degree, be a man! He should be able to choose what he wants to do, not like me. (*Looking at the shirt*) You know it all! When he was a kid and he talked back to his mother—I didn't want to hit him, so I made him go up to his room and sit at his desk, and write the word "respect"—about five hundred times, that was enough. (*He laughs*) Once I made him write it two thousand times. And that was the time he used carbon paper. He still wrote it a thousand times . . . but what was the point after he used the carbon paper? He's too big to hit. Now I couldn't do it anyway. Sometimes I'd like to. I don't know how to talk to him. (*He pauses*) That time he was a freshman. I went up to school to talk to him. It was his mother's idea. He didn't understand a thing I said. He thought I was saying that he was peculiar or something. But I didn't mean that! I wanted him to have a lot of friends, not just one. It pays to know a lot of people. That's all I meant! (*He pauses*) How could he think . . . I could think that? He's a good boy. He'll go back to school.

(*As the* FATHER *finishes his speech, the lights rise on the* YOUNG MAN *and the* GIRL. *Ghostly wailings and hootings are heard. Lights rise on a bed. A record player and some records scattered about are at one end of the bed. Notebooks and textbooks are at the other. The* YOUNG MAN *and the* GIRL *appear*)

YOUNG MAN   I am the ghost of Ground Hog's Day past, come to revenge my untimely demise.

13

GIRL   How did you demise?

YOUNG MAN   Very badly. I was trampled by a herd of stampeding ground hogs!

GIRL   How wise of you to come to me about it, Queen of the Druids. (*She stands, wrapped in the sheets*) Wait till you see this (*Adjusting the sheet*) Now. Is that sexy or is that sexy?

YOUNG MAN   Yes, I'd say it was very sexy. That's why you have to come back here right away.
            (*He reaches for her*)

GIRL   No-oo. I'm a druidess now. We are very pure.

YOUNG MAN   Look, you can still be pure, I promise.

GIRL   I know. It's a purifying thing.

YOUNG MAN   Right.

GIRL   Shall we have some music?

YOUNG MAN   Yes, some music, maestro, please.

GIRL   What do you want to hear?

YOUNG MAN   Play the Mozart.

GIRL   Our sonata?

14

YOUNG MAN   Yes.

GIRL (*She goes to the phonograph and puts the record on*) I bet we're the only people who have our own sonata. It's much nicer to say "our sonata," than to say, "the song they played at your mommy and daddy's wedding, Sonny, was 'September Song,' " or something.

YOUNG MAN   We will have Bach.

GIRL   And everyone will waltz.

YOUNG MAN   Waltz? No . . . I say there will be no wedding! We're going to elope to New England in jeans and a sweatshirt.

GIRL   That sounds beautiful. When can we go?

YOUNG MAN   As soon as I get my scholarship and the school makes me a boy millionaire.

GIRL   You'll get it. You're so good . . . they have to give it to you.

YOUNG MAN   And we can move into a big glass penthouse, away from this dump.

GIRL   I wonder who lived here before us. Do you think anyone was born or died here?

YOUNG MAN   Definitely died here. Eaten by cockroaches.

GIRL I think it's nice to be part of some historic context. That things were here before you . . . that there's some kind of continuity to things . . . that we're not isolated, unconnected . . . there's some security in that.

YOUNG MAN I think we're very secure.

GIRL I don't know. I sort of wish we could be frozen in time—right now—put on a Grecian urn. Did I ever tell you about this dream I had?

YOUNG MAN What dream?

GIRL I dreamt that you were a famous pianist, and you had all these big conductors and composers over for lunch one day, and I was sitting in this little room upstairs, by myself, making pottery.

YOUNG MAN Pottery?

GIRL It wasn't important.

YOUNG MAN Well, I wouldn't keep you in a back room. You'd be right out there with me, in some wild dress, and everyone would be gathered around you, thinking how beautiful you were.

GIRL Sometimes I can't see me fitting into your life. I think what it would be like if we met twenty years from now, and we were strangers. And you'd think, My, there's that girl I slept with when I was in school. She knew me as well as I did . . . but she doesn't know me any more.

YOUNG MAN   That won't happen. We'll never be strangers. (*He pauses*) Hey!

GIRL   What?

YOUNG MAN   How many kids are we going to have?

GIRL   I don't know.

YOUNG MAN   How many do you want?

GIRL   None right now.

YOUNG MAN   None? Well, I want twelve.

GIRL   Twelve!

YOUNG MAN   Yes. One for every month. We name all the girls after the spring and summer months, and all the boys after the fall and winter months.

GIRL   Here June, here July, here August . . .

YOUNG MAN (*They laugh, he holds her*)   And you're going to be a wonderful mother. And we'll take our babies to the park, and when they're older, we'll take them to concerts and museums.

GIRL   That'll be nice.

YOUNG MAN   Maybe they can come to my concerts, if I ever give any.

GIRL   You will. You'll be a great pianist, and we'll go all
over the world and you'll play with the greatest sym-
phonies.

YOUNG MAN   I'll have my hands insured by Lloyds of Lon-
don.

GIRL   What should I have insured?

YOUNG MAN   I'll show you.

GIRL   I know, I know, you don't have to show me . . . (*He
tickles her*) Stop it, stop it. (*Laughing, she falls off the
bed*) Oww. I hurt my elbow.

YOUNG MAN   Here, let me kiss it for you and make it better.

GIRL   It's all right. (*She pauses*) Do you really want twelve
children? That's a huge responsibility.
    (*Lights fade as the music continues to play*)

YOUNG MAN   At least twelve. One for every month. Then
maybe we'll start on the planets . . .

    (*The lights fade on the* YOUNG MAN. *We hear gunfire.
    Lights flash. Cross fade. Music out. Lights flash again.
    The* YOUNG MAN *runs back and forth. The* LITTLE BOY
    lies down under the tree, as if dead. A SOLDIER *walks
    slowly toward him. He wipes his forehead and drinks
    from a canteen. Then he calls*)

SOLDIER   Hey, you better come on over here. Hey, you hear
me? You better come over here.

YOUNG MAN (*He wears his dark clothes. He walks slowly to the tree. As he comes closer, he stands staring. The other* SOLDIER *walks away*) Oh, God. (*He whispers at first, then his voice breaks, rising*) Oh, God. I didn't mean to do it. It was an accident. I didn't mean to do it. (*To the* SOLDIER) They'll be all right. We'll take them to a hospital. (*To the* LITTLE BOY) You'll be all right. I promise. (*He holds the* LITTLE BOY) You'll be all right. (*He smoothes the* LITTLE BOY's *hair, tries to wipe the blood off him*) You'll be as good as new, I promise. And your mom and dad will be all right, too. When I was a boy, I was playing in a tree and I fell out of it and broke my arm. But see? (*He shows the* LITTLE BOY *his arm*) It's as good as new. Everything will be all right. I didn't mean to hurt you.
(*He hugs the* LITTLE BOY, *sits silent*)

SOLDIER (*Walking up to the* YOUNG MAN *and the* LITTLE BOY) Here. Fill these out.

YOUNG MAN What are they?

SOLDIER You know what they are. Put in the place and the date, and tie one on each of them. I said tie one on each of them. You made this mess, so fill them out.

YOUNG MAN All right. (*He takes the tags and a pen and tries to fill them out*) I can't seem to hold the pen. (*He tries to laugh*) Do you think you could help me?
(*The* SOLDIER *kneels down and finishes the tags*)

SOLDIER We're going to have to take them over there in that field so they can pick them up. I'll take that one. You get those two.

YOUNG MAN   You mean the mother and son.

SOLDIER   All right—the mother and son. Let's go.
(*The* SOLDIER *exits first. Then the* YOUNG MAN *attaches the tag to the* LITTLE BOY'*s wrist and carries him offstage. The* MOTHER *comes out. She kneels in front of the geraniums, weeding them. The* FATHER *enters, carrying a paper plate with a sandwich on it*)

FATHER   Here . . . I made you some lunch.

MOTHER   I was just going to come in and start something.

FATHER   It's tuna fish.

MOTHER   That's fine.

FATHER (*Pointing to the flowers*)   It looks good.

MOTHER   It looks the same as it's looked every year since we've lived here.

FATHER   Well, this year it looks especially nice.

MOTHER (*Looking up at him*)   I'm glad you like it.

FATHER (*Bending over*)   Geraniums.

MOTHER   Yes. (*She pauses*) They were his favorite flower.

FATHER   I didn't know that.

MOTHER   How many times did you ever talk about flowers with him?

FATHER   Not often.

MOTHER   They're terribly hard to keep. If they get too much sun or water, they'll die.

FATHER   What's so unusual about that? Sounds like all flowers to me.

MOTHER   They're just very delicate, that's all. You have to watch them a lot.

FATHER   All that work . . . hardly seems worth it. They don't bloom for very long, do they?
          (*If the* FATHER *is talking about his son, he doesn't know it*)

MOTHER   Not very.

FATHER   You going to pick them?

MOTHER   Pick them? Of course not.

FATHER   I thought you liked to pick flowers and bring them in the house.

MOTHER   Not these. These look the nicest right where they are.

FATHER   Good. I never liked picked flowers. You put them on the dining-room table and they wilt and die. Then you have to throw them out and bring in new ones.

MOTHER   You make it sound like it's my fault they die.
          (*She is not accusing him*)

FATHER   You pick them.
          (*He is kidding with her*)

MOTHER   Oh, come on. Would you rather have plastic plants? They never wilt . . . all you have to do is dust them off every few days.

FATHER   I like the wild flowers the best. Remember when I made you a dandelion bouquet?

MOTHER   Hardly! That must have been twenty years ago!

FATHER   I'll pick you another bouquet, if you like!
          (*He is courting her*)

MOTHER   Well, I'm not going to ask.

FATHER   All right! As soon as some come up, I'll pick you a whole bunch. I never knew these were his favorite flower. How come?

MOTHER   I don't know why . . . he just said it one day. Sometimes I pretend he's away at school. That helps.

FATHER   You shouldn't pretend like that.

MOTHER   You're away all week. I have to live here every day.

FATHER   I've asked you to come with me. We'd have time
to be alone . . . to talk and go out . . .

MOTHER   Now that would be pretending. (*She pauses*) I
have no reason to go with you when you're doing business,
really. I'd just be bored sitting around those strange towns
all day. Besides . . . what would happen when we had to
come home? If I did go away . . . I don't think I would
come back.

FATHER   Oh, the man from the PTA called me again. He
thought you had changed your mind.

MOTHER   Did you tell him I had not changed my mind?

FATHER   I said I'd ask you.

MOTHER   You can tell him to go to hell. (*She pauses*) And
leave us alone.

FATHER   (*He does not understand why she does not like the
idea*)   But they only want to have a program in his honor.
It's for him. The principal would be there, and his old
teachers . . .
      (*It is a kind explanation, a gentle plea*)

MOTHER   It's not for him . . . they only want to put us up
there on exhibit. So they can feel guilty about what's hap-
pening and pay for it with our loss.
      (*She is objective and to the point. But she is also kind.
It does not sound like a correction*)

23

FATHER   It wouldn't be anything like that. It's for him. And for us.

MOTHER   No it isn't.

FATHER   He would have liked it.

MOTHER   He would not.

FATHER   (*Losing his temper and destroying his attempt to make his wife feel better*)   Why? Because you don't like it? If you'd have had your way you would have kept him in a glass bowl, on the dining-room table, just like the flowers.

MOTHER   Better than where he is!

FATHER   (*Pauses*)   I'll tell him no. I'm sorry I mentioned it. I thought you'd like it.

MOTHER   (*Forgiving*)   It's all right.

FATHER   (*Knowing he is asking for the impossible. He must say it anyway, so he kids*)   You know, if this tree weren't here, we'd have a beautiful view from the house.
   (*Again he does not know he is talking about his son*)

MOTHER   (*Knowing what he really wants, and knowing they both know he isn't going to get it*)   And a nice place to shoot golf balls?

FATHER   Well, that too . . .

24

David Birney as the YOUNG MAN and
Blythe Danner as the GIRL.

MOTHER   The tree stays right where it is!
(*Her mood is good again*)

FATHER   Oh, it's so old it's probably dead!
(*This is the last resort*)

MOTHER   It is not and you know it! You just want a golf course!

FATHER   And you're just out to save your flower bed!

MOTHER   (*Laughs, then pauses, remembering*) You're darn right! Besides, I like this tree. Do you remember—

FATHER   Here we go! You're going to pull some old sentimental story on me . . . you can keep the tree!

MOTHER   No, I was just thinking of the time we all built the tree house.

FATHER   It wasn't a tree house. It was a lookout tower.
(*He is one-upping her*)

MOTHER   (*One-upping him back*) It was a secret hideout-lookout tower combination.

FATHER   (*Sticking to his version*)   I remember that lookout tower. The whole thing fell down with him in it!

MOTHER   My heart must have stopped beating. I had no idea that was going to happen.

FATHER All I know is we were laughing so hard . . .

MOTHER (*She knows they were laughing*) We were not laughing!

FATHER Yes we were! He looked so funny when the whole thing fell down.

MOTHER There was nothing funny about his breaking his arm.

FATHER We weren't laughing at that! It was almost eleven years ago.

MOTHER Eleven years ago this summer.

FATHER Everything looks the same. As if time had stopped and the world never touched us.

MOTHER (*Quietly*) Never touched us . . .

FATHER It's like we're right back where we started, twenty-three years ago.

MOTHER (*She starts to walk off. She is talking more to herself than to her husband*) And the whole thing only cost us my son.
    (*She leaves. The* FATHER *follows her off with his eyes. Then he goes to the garden, kneels down and touches the geranium*)

LITTLE BOY (*From offstage*) Dad!

FATHER (*Not sure he is hearing*) What?

LITTLE BOY Dad!
(*He enters, carrying a large board which he drags behind him*)

FATHER Hi, buddy! What's that for?

LITTLE BOY I'm going to build a lookout tower.

FATHER (*To himself, proud he remembered correctly*) It *was* a lookout tower! (*To the* LITTLE BOY) Well, you're gonna need a lot more wood than that. Where are you going to build it?

LITTLE BOY Up in the tree. Will you help?

FATHER Well, hell, that's an awful lot of work. I don't think we could get it finished today, and I have to go away in the morning . . .

LITTLE BOY But Mom said you'd help me if I asked you.

FATHER If you want me to help you, you can ask me, not your mother. (*The* LITTLE BOY *whines to himself and sits down under the tree*) I was thinking of cutting that branch. What do you think?

LITTLE BOY Dad . . . (*Pause; they look at each other*) Will you toss ball with me?

27

FATHER Well, sure! Go get your glove and a ball and we'll go a few innings. (*He tickles the* LITTLE BOY *as he runs by him, then calls after him*) You know where that new glove is I bought you?

LITTLE BOY Yeah!

FATHER I bet you never even used it. (*He walks about the tree, talking to himself*) What's he going to do with a lookout tower! He'd sit up there all day by himself . . . rot the summer away doing nothing. Between practicing the piano and going to the orthodontist . . .

LITTLE BOY Dad . . .

FATHER Let's see the ball. Hey, a hardball.

LITTLE BOY I couldn't find the softball.

FATHER Going to play for real, huh? Well, we won't say anything to your mother.

LITTLE BOY (*Smiling*) Okay.

FATHER All right now. Let's see you powder one over here. (*The* LITTLE BOY *throws the ball badly, trying to make it hard and fast*) When is the last time you threw a ball? Okay. Let's see your windup . . . nice and loose . . . Flip your wrist and follow through. Got it?

LITTLE BOY I think so.

FATHER   Okay, let's try it. (*They back apart*) Toss it over here! (*It goes over the* FATHER's *head, offstage. He runs after it, returns*) No control! You didn't watch where you were throwing it!
(MOTHER *enters as* FATHER *is offstage*)

LITTLE BOY   Hi, Mom!

MOTHER   How you doing?

FATHER   Fine. All he needs is a little practice.
(*He throws the ball hard*)

LITTLE BOY   Ow! You're hurting my hand.

MOTHER   Is that a hardball?

LITTLE BOY   Yes. So what?
(*He is stopping the game*)

MOTHER   I told you not to use a hardball. If he got hit in the mouth . . .

FATHER   Leave him alone. He's not going to get hit.

MOTHER   No. Give me that ball and get a softball.

LITTLE BOY   Why don't you stay out of this?

MOTHER   Now listen here . . . go get a softball!

LITTLE BOY   I don't know where one is.
(*He gives her the ball*)

MOTHER   So look for it. I thought you two were going to build a lookout tower.

LITTLE BOY   Dad didn't want to.

FATHER   What's he going to do with a lookout tower? Tossing ball is better for him.

MOTHER   I'll tell you what. We'll all build the lookout tower. How's that?

FATHER   For one thing, that tree isn't going to hold a tree house.

MOTHER   Sure it will. It might not hold you . . .

FATHER   All right—

MOTHER   But it certainly is big enough to hold him!

FATHER   What the hell is he going to do up there? Sit with a shotgun and pick off the neighbors?

LITTLE BOY   It can be a hideout . . .

FATHER   Who you hiding from?

MOTHER   Come on, let's build the thing. We have to get nails and hammers too . . . I'll help carry it out. (MOTHER *and the* LITTLE BOY *start to leave*) Are you coming?

FATHER   Yes, I'm coming.

(MOTHER *and the* LITTLE BOY *exit.* FATHER *stands looking at the tree. He walks off in an opposite direction than that of the* MOTHER *and the* LITTLE BOY. *Lights rise on the tree. The* YOUNG MAN *and a* SOLDIER *sit beneath the tree. They are both reading letters. The* YOUNG MAN *finishes reading his, and puts it back in the envelope. Then he puts it in his pocket. He looks at the* SOLDIER, *who is still reading, so he takes his letter out, opens the envelope and rereads it*)

YOUNG MAN   Are you still reading your letter? I've read mine two and a half times already.

SOLDIER   I've read mine two and a half times already too.

YOUNG MAN   Oh. What's new at home?

SOLDIER   Nothing. Nothing's ever new.

YOUNG MAN   Is it from your girl?

SOLDIER   No, it's . . . from my mama.

YOUNG MAN   So's mine. All she ever writes is that I don't write enough.

SOLDIER   Yeah, mine too. I try to explain to her that I'm busy.

YOUNG MAN   That never works on mine. She says, "You can't be so busy that you can't spare five minutes just to write a line and say you're all right." But five minutes is a damn long time. Too long to waste. Think what can happen in five minutes.

SOLDIER   Think what can happen in one minute.

YOUNG MAN   That's right. Or even in a couple of seconds. One lousy second.

SOLDIER   That's all it takes.

YOUNG MAN   Five minutes. Can you think of how many times in your life five minutes has changed everything? I don't mean like missing a bus or anything. Like, maybe you wouldn't have met your girl friend. Or what if your parents had missed each other by five minutes? You wouldn't even be here.

(*The* GIRL *enters and sits stage right*)

SOLDIER   No shit!

GIRL   When I first met you, you really scared me. It was in English class . . .

YOUNG MAN   I remember when I first met my girl at home . . .

GIRL   You changed seats so you could sit next to me.

YOUNG MAN   We were seniors in high school . . .

SOLDIER   And horny as the dickens . . .

32

GIRL   And you said, "Hi, you don't know me, but I know you." You invited me to your birthday party once . . . and you told me I looked the same as I had when we were nine and I laughed . . . I think because you scared me. And I didn't remember you. Then you asked me out.

YOUNG MAN   For a long time she wouldn't go out with me. I don't blame her.

GIRL   Honest to God, I thought you were the most amazing creep. I hated to go to English class!

YOUNG MAN   How it really got started was I'd write her these notes, and after a while she started to write back. They developed into this epic masterpiece. They'd be amazing wild stories . . . like how her mother had a furniture store in the Belgian Congo . . . she specialized in Congo Colonial. We went to visit her and had all these run-ins with wild crazy people.

GIRL   Remember the story about that boy? . . . I can't remember his name . . . you know, the one who drove the Thunderbird to school every day? We locked him in the trunk of his car and sold them both to the gypsies—who just happened to be in town.

YOUNG MAN   And then they were going to take the car back to Rumania and sell it to the Communists, who would be able to sabotage the Ford Motor Company . . .

GIRL   But the steamer went down in a storm . . .

33

YOUNG MAN And that guy locked in the trunk of his Thunderbird drowned . . .

GIRL Along with the chemistry teacher, who had a specially treated exploding tie . . .

YOUNG MAN I can't remember exactly how the chemistry teacher got on the gypsy steamer.

GIRL The first time I loved you . . . sort of—it was all very high-schoolish—was when we were working together on the state science project.

YOUNG MAN Do you know what we were doing? It was really a wild idea. It was for botany class, so we took leaves from all the rare, exotic trees in the neighborhood . . . (*He rises and picks a leaf from a tree branch*) and we pressed them in plastic!

GIRL We saw this article in *Scientific American* on how to do it. You heat the plastic square with the leaf on it and something heavy on top for pressure, and it leaves an imprint in the plastic. Wasn't that something?

YOUNG MAN Preserved forever in plastic.

GIRL I remember we were working on it down in my basement. First thing you know we were rolling around on the cement floor, making-out like mad.

YOUNG MAN (*To the* SOLDIER) I guess I'd better answer my mother's letter. I haven't written in a long time.

SOLDIER I'll write mine tonight.

YOUNG MAN Letters. What a desperate way to hold onto people.

GIRL At first we wrote to each other a lot. As much as we could. But then I said to myself that we'd been pretending long enough. There was nothing left of what used to be, and a lot of letters didn't make up for anything. So I started dating other guys and there were some I . . . wanted to go to bed with. But when they would touch me, I'd think of him . . . touching me. And I couldn't do it. I wrote him less, and finally, not at all. But he kept writing me. Always. Even now I'll find myself pretending like we used to, pretending . . . that he's still here . . . and I don't know what to do.
(She exits)

YOUNG MAN Boy, do I wish I had a piano here right now! I'd pound out the greatest Beethoven sonata you ever heard!
(He plays the ground as if it were a piano)

SOLDIER I hope you shoot better than you play.

YOUNG MAN I don't.

SOLDIER If you ask me, you're practicing the wrong thing.
(He exits. The lights rise on the YOUNG MAN. He is in his room; a suitcase lies on the bed. He is packing)

35

MOTHER   Hi. Can I help?

YOUNG MAN   No, it's okay. I'm only taking overnight stuff.

MOTHER   Well, take enough socks and underwear.

YOUNG MAN   They give you that stuff—I don't have to bring it.

MOTHER   All right . . . I don't want to sound like a mother.

YOUNG MAN   Well, I got big news . . . you do!

MOTHER   I can't help it . . . but just think—you won't have to hear my nagging for two years.

YOUNG MAN   Yeah, isn't that amazing? What do you think I'll die of first? Exposure or malnutrition?

MOTHER   Neither. Just eat enough and dress warm.

YOUNG MAN   God! You're such a mother!

MOTHER   I just don't want you getting sick.

YOUNG MAN   If I didn't think that . . . that I could take care of myself . . . I doubt I could go where I'm going.

MOTHER   You'll do fine. I know you can take care of yourself—I'm only teasing.

YOUNG MAN You mothers are all alike—you're no damned good.

MOTHER We're a rotten bunch, we are.

YOUNG MAN Yeah.

MOTHER But just don't you go writing how terrible the food is . . . after all the complaining you've done, you deserve it!

YOUNG MAN I never once complained about your cooking! It's that my clothes are falling apart.

MOTHER Now I'm a negligent mother!

YOUNG MAN I didn't say that . . . on the whole, I think you were an outstanding mother. You raised me admirably!

MOTHER Thank you . . . (*Looking for words*) I . . . well, I want to tell you not to worry . . . everything . . .

YOUNG MAN I know . . . you don't have to say anything.

MOTHER All right.

YOUNG MAN I'm sure it'll all be very glamorous and exciting, if I can learn to point a gun at somebody and shoot them.

MOTHER I guess they teach you how.

YOUNG MAN Teach me what? Do you really have to learn things like that?

MOTHER Don't think about it. Just say it's not you doing those things. Somebody else sent you there and they're using you to do what they want . . .

YOUNG MAN But I can't think that! I'm me!

MOTHER You'll be all right.

YOUNG MAN Dad says the best soldier is a scared soldier. I should be fantastic.

MOTHER You don't have to be fantastic. Just . . . You'll be all right. I promise.

LITTLE BOY (*He appears, calling, in a spot, stage right*) Mom! Mom!
    (MOTHER *turns her head toward the voice, then away*)

MOTHER What is it?

LITTLE BOY Dad said I have to go to camp. I don't want to go.

MOTHER Do we have to go through this each summer? You act like we're sending you to jail.

LITTLE BOY But I don't like it.

MOTHER When you get out there you know you'll have a good time. It's good for you.
    (*The* YOUNG MAN *goes to his dresser and looks to backstage*)

38

LITTLE BOY   I won't go. I hate it. They make me do things I don't like.

MOTHER   Sometimes you have to do things you don't like. And most of the time they're good for you.

LITTLE BOY   Did you go to camp?

MOTHER   No. My parents couldn't afford to send me. You're lucky we can.

LITTLE BOY   I wish you couldn't afford it!

MOTHER (*Laughs at him*)   You're so silly! It's not the end of the world.

FATHER (*Enters and speaks to the* YOUNG MAN)   How's it going?

YOUNG MAN   Fine. Not much to do.

LITTLE BOY   But why won't you let me stay here?

FATHER   Good.
(*He pats him on the back*)

MOTHER   Because we all could use a rest. That's what a vacation means. To get away.

FATHER   It won't be long now.

YOUNG MAN   No, I guess not.

LITTLE BOY   But I don't want to go away. Why can't I go with Dad?

MOTHER   You can go with your father some other time.

MOTHER (*To the* YOUNG MAN)   How you used to hate to go to camp!

YOUNG MAN   I even remember me and this other kid ran away, and they sent the police out looking for us . . .

FATHER   He'd ask me to take him with me—just to get out of it.

YOUNG MAN   It wasn't just to get out of it. I really wanted to go with you.

MOTHER   It seems like we're sending you off to summer camp again.

YOUNG MAN   I almost wish you were.

FATHER   You're doing a good thing, whether you know it or not, and you'll be a better person for it.

YOUNG MAN   I wasn't exactly thinking about that right now. But you always seem to bring it up.

FATHER   Well, that's what you should be thinking about.

YOUNG MAN   If you want to know the truth, I was considering the possibilities of running away again.

FATHER   You just try it and see what happens to you.

MOTHER (*To* FATHER)   He's only teasing you . . .

FATHER (*To the* YOUNG MAN)   He'll do just fine. He'll make us proud of him.

YOUNG MAN   I have enough problems without worrying about making you proud of me.

MOTHER   We are proud of you.

YOUNG MAN   That's nice to know.

FATHER   Do you need me for anything? If not, I've got some work to do.

MOTHER   Not right now.
       (FATHER *looks at the* YOUNG MAN *and walks out*)

YOUNG MAN   He's always got to put the pressure on.

MOTHER   He didn't mean it. You don't have to be so mean to him.

YOUNG MAN   I wasn't being mean. Why is his being proud of me something I have to keep winning, over and over? I hate to think what he expects me to do this time.

MOTHER   He was never tough on himself. He doesn't want to see you make the same . . .

YOUNG MAN   I know the story.

41

MOTHER Then if you know it, try to understand. And stop fighting with him.

YOUNG MAN There's a war in the family. Tell him to stop fighting with me.

MOTHER You must be very glad you're getting away.

YOUNG MAN You just think that. (*They are silent. The* YOUNG MAN *walks to his dresser and unfolds a pair of socks. He puts his hand in a sock. His thumb sticks out of a hole. He calls to his* MOTHER) Do you think I could borrow a pair of Dad's socks? All mine have holes in them.
     (*Bach music starts. He walks slowly to the tree and sits down. He peels the sock off his hand very slowly, as if it were skin. He grimaces in pain.*)

Black out

Act Two

ACT TWO

The YOUNG MAN *is sitting, leaning against the tree. He rises, walks forward.*

YOUNG MAN You see this tree? This tree has been here for years and years. When I was a boy, I used to think that it was an old man, and that at night, after I was asleep, he'd walk around the back yard, or come look in my window. I even thought that these two knots on his trunk were his eyes—and that he was watching me. I used to put my arms around him—well, not very far around him—and listen for his heartbeat. But I never could hear it. I was sure he was alive though, and anything that was alive had to have a heart, so I knew he had one someplace. I can feel my heart, *(He touches his chest)* in my wrists and on my eyelids. The skin is very soft here, over my heart. So soft, the skin separated as easily as spreading your fingers when the knife stuck in. The skin parted so easily that it seemed as if nothing were ever holding it together. The blood comes out like mad—like water out of a garden hose. First in bursts and spurts, then flowing, flowing. It dries brown. Sticky and hard—a giant scab. It smells terrible. You feel your eyelids and your wrists and there's nothing there. You squeeze . . . and you get scared because there's nothing there! There . . . *(The* LITTLE BOY *comes out, unseen by the* YOUNG MAN, *howls and falls to the ground. The* YOUNG MAN *spins around, terrified. He sees the* LITTLE BOY *with a small kitchen knife slipped in between the buttons of his shirt, ketchup splashed generously over his shirt. The* YOUNG MAN *runs over to the* LITTLE BOY, *then looks down and sees he has been tricked*) A kitchen knife and some ketchup! (*The* LITTLE BOY *laughs uproariously*) Goddamn you, you scared me to death! (*The* LITTLE BOY *continues laughing. The* YOUNG MAN *stares at him silently and lets him laugh himself out*) I don't think it's one bit funny.

LITTLE BOY   You should have seen how scared you looked.

YOUNG MAN   Well, I was scared! You would have been too.

LITTLE BOY   You should have seen what happened this morning.

YOUNG MAN   You mean you've been running around doing this all day?

LITTLE BOY   Yeah, except for lunch.

YOUNG MAN   That's wonderful.

LITTLE BOY   I tried it on the corner across from the drug store. (*The* YOUNG MAN *shakes his head*) It was really neat. These two old ladies—

YOUNG MAN   Oh no!

LITTLE BOY   One of them screamed!

YOUNG MAN   You're an idiot! You could have given them a heart attack.

LITTLE BOY   No . . . as soon as the one screamed I started laughing. Then the other one grabbed my arm and said she was going to call the police.

YOUNG MAN   So I bet you ran like hell.

LITTLE BOY   You're not kidding.

YOUNG MAN   How many people have you done this to already?

LITTLE BOY   There were a couple more. But most of the people just walked right on by. A couple of them laughed because they saw what I was doing; but some of them went across the street so they wouldn't have to walk by me. It sure was funny.

YOUNG MAN   I think it's pretty stupid. Don't you ever do anything worthwhile?

LITTLE BOY   I go to school!

YOUNG MAN   Of course. I forgot. So how's school? Do you like it?

LITTLE BOY   It's all right.

YOUNG MAN   The thing that I liked best about school was getting out. Especially for things you weren't expecting. Do they still have fire drills and air raid warnings? We were always getting rushed off to the playground for fires, or down to the basement for air raids.

LITTLE BOY We have fire drills. I've been waiting for the school to burn down since third grade.

YOUNG MAN I wonder if we ever realized what we were all doing down there in the basement, lined up along the walls with our arms over our heads . . . waiting. God. What a thing to practice!

LITTLE BOY Why'd they put you in the basement? The whole school would fall down on you.

YOUNG MAN Yeah, I thought about that too. What a strange thing to grow up with, thinking you could get blown up. When you accept something like that as being ordinary when you're in grade school, what do you think's ordinary when you're grown up?

LITTLE BOY But it got you out of school, didn't it? That's what's important.

YOUNG MAN Hey, look at that ant carrying that little piece of food.

LITTLE BOY It's bigger than the ant.

YOUNG MAN Ants expect that of each other. They don't think anything of it. (*They watch the ant silently, their faces together and close to the ground*) Look at him go.

LITTLE BOY Where's he going?

YOUNG MAN Home to the wife and kids, I guess.

48

LITTLE BOY   How does he know which ants are his wife and kids? They all look the same.

YOUNG MAN   He must have some way of telling. (*Stretches, lies on his back*) Good old summertime!

LITTLE BOY (*Stretches, lies on his back just like the* YOUNG MAN) Good old summertime!

YOUNG MAN (*Sitting up, cross-legged*)   Doing anything this summer?

LITTLE BOY (*Sitting up, cross-legged, just like the* YOUNG MAN) No.

YOUNG MAN   Not even Little League?

LITTLE BOY   Maybe next year.

YOUNG MAN   Well, where'd all your friends go? . . .

LITTLE BOY   I don't know.

YOUNG MAN   'Cause whenever I see you, you're always by yourself.

LITTLE BOY   *No* I'm not, I'm with you!

YOUNG MAN   That's right! Well, I guess we should do something, long as we're both sitting here doing nothing. (*He pauses*) How about a boost into the tree? It's a great lookout tower.

49

LITTLE BOY   Yeah, okay.

YOUNG MAN   Here you go! (*He helps the* LITTLE BOY *up into the tree*) Hold tight. Got it?

LITTLE BOY   Okay!

YOUNG MAN   What can you see?

LITTLE BOY   Everything. The whole world! Hey, there's the school!

YOUNG MAN   Tell me what's going on, what I'm missing.

LITTLE BOY   There's the Dairy Queen, and the cemetery.

YOUNG MAN   Sounds like everything's the same since I was up there.

LITTLE BOY   Come on up!

YOUNG MAN   No, that's okay. Why don't you come down? It's getting late.

LITTLE BOY   I'll jump!

YOUNG MAN   No, just climb down. Don't be a show-off. (*The* LITTLE BOY *climbs down*)

LITTLE BOY   It's really fun up there.

YOUNG MAN   I knew you'd like it.

LITTLE BOY   We're best friends, aren't we?

YOUNG MAN   Yes!

LITTLE BOY   That's good.
      (*Both exit. As lights fade on the* YOUNG MAN *and the*
      LITTLE BOY, *a light rises on the* MOTHER)

MOTHER (*To the audience*)   You know, when it comes, you
think it's going to be a terrible surprise, that you'll tear it
up or wad it into a little ball, that you'll scream or go in-
sane. Or at least cry. But you don't. You know it's happened before the telegram arrives. Something in your mind
heard the clicks of the teletype machine addressing you as
"Dear Mr. and Mrs. So-and-so," and adding its deep-felt
regrets, before you even see the paper. I went out in the
backyard and sat down in the grass under the tree. It's been
years since I've sat in the grass. So I sat there and I thought
back to when we had this Irish setter . . . her name was
Ginger. Her full name was Gingerella of Brianwood—the
only royalty I've ever met. It was funny to be thinking
about an old dog at a time like that, but that's what I was
thinking. I remembered how I used to pretend I was crying because it would upset her. She'd run over and jump
on me—and she was a very big dog—and she'd whine and
lick my face. She really thought I was crying. Then I
would burst out laughing and push her away. One day she
got sick and I had to take her to the vet. He said she
would have to stay there, and to take her upstairs where he
had a room full of cages where he kept the dogs. Ginger
was so sick she could hardly get up the stairs. I tried to
help her, but all my pushing and pulling probably hurt her

more. When we got into the room, all the dogs started barking and jumping around. It scared Ginger and she tried to run away. But she could hardly move. So she just cried. I led her into her cage and then I ran down those stairs, so glad to be away from there. I never saw Ginger again. She died, and I guess they tossed her into an incinerator somewhere. I never cried until that day in the backyard. (*Pause*) And I don't even know if I was crying for Ginger . . . or my son.

(*She exits. Fadeout. Lights rise on the* YOUNG MAN *and the* FATHER. *They walk in from stage left*)

FATHER This okay?

YOUNG MAN Fine, great! (*They sit down*) I'm just so surprised to see you here. I had no idea you were coming.

FATHER Good to see you too, buddy. Ever come out here before?

YOUNG MAN No, this is the first time. How could I get here? I don't have a car.

FATHER Don't worry about that. Be patient. As soon as I can afford it . . .

YOUNG MAN No, really, Dad, it's okay. I wasn't asking for a car. In fact, I'd rather buy it myself.

FATHER You need money for that.

YOUNG MAN So I'll get a job.

FATHER   Well, I'm glad to see you're willing to work for something you want . . .

YOUNG MAN   I don't know how we got into this . . . but I don't even want a car . . .

FATHER   Well, if you did want it, you'd work for it.

YOUNG MAN   Of course.

FATHER   That's all that counts. So. How's school?

YOUNG MAN   It's there.

FATHER   What's that supposed to mean? You're bored.

YOUNG MAN   I have a very low threshold for boredom.

FATHER   You wouldn't be bored if you got into your work and stopped piddling around. If you're busy you don't have time to be bored.

YOUNG MAN   Aren't you ever bored with your job? I would be.

FATHER   No. I don't have time to be bored.

YOUNG MAN   Do you think you would be if you had the time?

FATHER   There's nothing funny about working. I have you and your mother to support. You can't laugh at your responsibilities.

YOUNG MAN   I don't mean to laugh at it—it's just that I'm not happy with what I'm taking. I don't care about three-fourths of the stuff. I'd rather be practicing the piano.

FATHER   You're not going to make any money playing the piano. All you could do would be to become a piano teacher.

YOUNG MAN   Not if I'm good. I know it'll take a long time, and you don't get money or recognition for years, if you get it at all . . .

FATHER   Well, if you know what the score—

YOUNG MAN   But it's what I want to do.

FATHER   You can't always do what you want to do. Look, buddy, I know what it's like. But you have to stop fooling yourself. You can't pretend that all you have to do is float around, doing what you feel like . . . having adventures. Look, I wanted to be a doctor. It was my big dream. But that's all I did about it. Dream. So I'm a salesman. But I'm the Goddamned best salesman the firm has, and I make as much money as most doctors.

YOUNG MAN   I know how hard you work.

FATHER   It keeps me away from your mother over half of every week, but if I didn't work as hard as I do, we couldn't live like we do.

YOUNG MAN   I didn't say anything about you and Mom. You don't have to defend yourself.

FATHER   I'm not defending myself. I'm trying to tell you that people get tied down. You don't want to be, but you do. You're a victim of what you are. It doesn't matter who you are—if you're nice or good-looking or intelligent—no matter who you are you have an obligation. A responsibility. Yours is to get good grades so you can be something when you get out of here. I don't care if you don't want to be a doctor, but Goddamnit, son, you're going to be something.

YOUNG MAN   The trouble is I'm not doing anything completely. I don't give school my whole effort, and I don't give practicing a whole effort either. I'm trying to please you and myself, and I'm not doing either.

FATHER   It's your decision.

YOUNG MAN   But I can't make it!

FATHER   I don't see why you couldn't do both if you worked harder.

YOUNG MAN   All right, I'll try . . .

FATHER   (*Caresses the* YOUNG MAN's *cheek with his hand*) Hey, buddy! You forgot to shave.

YOUNG MAN   I didn't forget. I just didn't feel like it. That's a nice thing about school. You can be a bum and nobody cares.

FATHER   Why don't you dress like a businessman? You've got a job to do. You have enough clothes?

YOUNG MAN   Everything's fine. Don't worry.

FATHER   Just get through with school. I don't want you being a perennial freshman.

YOUNG MAN   I'm almost a sophomore.

FATHER   You know what I mean. (*He pauses*) There's something I came up to talk to you about. Your mother spoke to me about it first and suggested I make the trip up.

YOUNG MAN   Is there something the matter?

FATHER   It's about you and your roommate.

YOUNG MAN   What?

FATHER   Your mother is worried that you and he . . . I don't know how to put it so you won't accuse us of prying into your life . . .

YOUNG MAN   Worried that what?

FATHER   She says you're . . . too close. That you live together at school and you're together at home all the vacation . . .

YOUNG MAN   He's my best friend! Of course I'm with him a lot.

FATHER   But not to the exclusion of everybody else.

YOUNG MAN   But nobody is being excluded. I don't have that many friends . . .

FATHER   You should be out making new friends, people that can help you later on . . .

YOUNG MAN   I don't make friends with people for what they can do for me.

FATHER   There's nothing wrong with that. You can never tell when you might need somebody's help.

YOUNG MAN   Haven't you ever liked someone just because of what they are, not for what they can do for you?

FATHER   There's enough time for that later. You should be out meeting people that can help you with your career. (*He pauses*) I thought we could look at apartments this week-end. I'd drive up Sunday . . .

YOUNG MAN   I won't do this. I won't! He's my best friend.

FATHER   As soon as you can get out . . .

YOUNG MAN   I can't do this to him. What can I tell him? It'd be the most disgusting thing I've ever done.

FATHER   Then don't tell him anything. And don't see him any more.

YOUNG MAN   What did Mom say to you?

FATHER   She said she doesn't like it that you're so insep-
arable. You're with him constantly at school, and when
you're home you can't wait to go over to his house . . .

YOUNG MAN   And she said you should come up here and tell
me to move out? . . .

FATHER   She said she wanted me to talk to you. Look, I don't
want you to see this boy any more! It'll be the easiest
way . . .

YOUNG MAN   You think I'm queer, don't you?

FATHER   Don't be ridiculous . . . What are you—

YOUNG MAN   I can't stand talking about this any more. I'll do
whatever you want. Just leave me alone.

FATHER   You can't get so attached to people, buddy. I don't
care what kind of attachment it is. You wouldn't have ben-
efited from this friendship. This kid doesn't even have the
advantages you've got.

YOUNG MAN   I said I'd do what you wanted, okay?

FATHER   You'll see it's the best thing. Know a lot of people.
Different, interesting people. People than can—

YOUNG MAN   All right! I said I'd do what you wanted!

FATHER   Keep your voice down.

58

YOUNG MAN   You just won't stop saying the same thing, over and over.

FATHER   We just want what's best for you. I know you've heard it a hundred times, and you'll never believe it, but it's true.

YOUNG MAN   You made your point.

FATHER   All right. When are you coming home again?

YOUNG MAN   I don't know.

FATHER   Next week? The week after?

YOUNG MAN   I have a lot of work to do. Probably not for a couple of weeks.

FATHER   Write your mother in the meantime, will you?

YOUNG MAN   I just wrote her.

FATHER   You wrote her two weeks ago. I saw the letter. You can do better than that.

YOUNG MAN   I don't have anything to say. Nothing happens.

FATHER   She misses you.

YOUNG MAN   I'll call her Sunday.

FATHER It's expensive. (*The* YOUNG MAN *glares at him*) It's not the same as writing.

YOUNG MAN Okay, Dad.

FATHER How's your girl friend? Same one?

YOUNG MAN Yes, same one. She's fine.

FATHER Getting along all right?

YOUNG MAN Yes, fine. Everything's fine.

FATHER I'm glad. You're pretty serious, aren't you?

YOUNG MAN Yes, I suppose.

FATHER You're lucky you both came to the same school. It's a lot more . . . convenient . . . for you.

YOUNG MAN (*Surprised, then covering it*) Yes.

FATHER Tell her I said hello.

YOUNG MAN I will. She likes you. Are you going back right away?

FATHER I wanted to start back as soon as I could, before it gets dark.

YOUNG MAN Couldn't you stay . . . just for dinner?

60

FATHER   Well, sure, buddy, I'd love to take you to dinner. I thought maybe you had plans . . .

YOUNG MAN   Well, even if I did, I'd have broken them.

FATHER   Well, let's go someplace nice for dinner.

YOUNG MAN   I hardly get to see you.

FATHER   What are you in the mood for?

YOUNG MAN   Can I have a steak?

FATHER   You can have whatever you want. You look like a skeleton. Don't you eat enough?

YOUNG MAN   The food stinks.

FATHER   Then go out and eat dinner. You have enough money?

YOUNG MAN   Yes. Everything's fine.

FATHER   Then let's put on a few pounds. Your mother'll scream if she sees you looking like this. (*Puts his arm around his son*) Are we still friends?

YOUNG MAN   Yes, we're still friends.

FATHER   Well, then let's say it with a little enthusiasm.

YOUNG MAN   I said it!

61

FATHER (*Holds his son so he can't get away and tickles him. They are both laughing*) What?

YOUNG MAN (*Laughing, hardly able to speak*) I said it!

FATHER (*Laughing*) Then say it again!

YOUNG MAN We're still friends!

FATHER (*Releasing him*) That's better!

YOUNG MAN God, you tickle so hard!

FATHER But it works.

YOUNG MAN It hurts!

FATHER Played any golf?

YOUNG MAN Not since I went out with you.

FATHER Don't you like it?

YOUNG MAN I don't know. It's sort of boring.

FATHER Not if you're good. A couple of more times out with me—

YOUNG MAN A couple of more times out with you like the last time, and I'll break every one of my clubs. As far as you were concerned, I didn't do a thing right!

FATHER I didn't say you didn't do a thing right. You just did a lot of things wrong. It'll never hurt to know how to play. It's good exercise and its good business.

YOUNG MAN Everything with you is business.

FATHER Yes, sir.

YOUNG MAN All right. We'd better go eat if you want to get back early.
(*They start to walk off*)

FATHER We'll get you that steak. And a baked potato and sour cream . . .

YOUNG MAN Sounds great! It seems like ten years since I've had a steak. If I never see a hamburger and French fries again, I honestly won't miss them.

FATHER Then we'd better get you two steaks!

YOUNG MAN I could eat them. I'm starving!

FATHER (*Grabs his son by the shoulders, shaking him affectionately*) I believe it, buddy, I believe it!

(*They walk off. The lights rise on the* GIRL. *She is sitting on the bed, listening to a small tape recorder. The Prelude and Fugue XII in F minor by Bach is playing. The piano plays as though each note were a carefully weighed and timed little drop. When the fugue ends, the* GIRL *turns off the tape recorder. It is raining outside. The wind is blowing as in a storm, and rain is falling against the windows. Records and books are scattered at each end of the bed as before. The bed is made. The room is dark. The fugue plays and the* GIRL *is sitting perfectly still. The* YOUNG MAN *comes in in a raincoat. He is wet, his hair is matted. The* GIRL *immediately gets up and goes to him and hugs him. He is not completely responding*)

YOUNG MAN   Hi! You'll get all wet!

GIRL   It's beautiful, it's so beautiful! I've listened to it a dozen times. Thank you. (*He smiles, takes off his raincoat*) No one's ever given me a *fugue* before. (*They laugh*) A little roll of tape in a ribbon with a note saying, "Play me, I'm yours."

YOUNG MAN   Sit down . . . I have to talk to you. It's about the scholarship.

GIRL   What? They're not going to give it to you!

YOUNG MAN   No.

GIRL   Why? Why?

YOUNG MAN   You won't believe me when I tell you. When they told me I laughed, I just sat there and laughed and said, "You're kidding," or something. My family has too much money for me to get a scholarship. Even if I had the grades, which I don't.

64

GIRL But didn't you tell them . . .

YOUNG MAN Yes, I gave them the whole story. I said, "But my father won't pay for me if I transfer to the School of Music full time." So the man said I should stay where I was so long as he was willing to pay for that. Goddamn. If their money doesn't get you one way, it gets you another. Can you believe how ludicrous this is? When he told me I just sat there and laughed.

GIRL Maybe your parents will change their minds. (*Pause*) I'm sorry. I knew how stupid it sounded before I'd even finished . . .

YOUNG MAN All I want to do is play the piano . . . and love you and have twelve kids.

GIRL Why not? Quit school. Work part time and take some courses at the School of Music.

YOUNG MAN I would, except I'd get drafted. That's all.

GIRL Then you'd better stay in school, I guess.

YOUNG MAN I don't know. I don't know what to do. If I don't do what I think is right, I'll wind up someplace I never wanted to go, doing something I don't want to be doing . . . which is what I'm doing now.

GIRL But it's not something you can't change later, that you can't make better.

YOUNG MAN My father wants me to be a man, and he'll do everything he can to prevent me from being one.

GIRL He isn't trying to hurt you, you know damned well he isn't. Your idea of a man and his . . .

YOUNG MAN He'll force me to stay in school and become what he wants me to be, or he'll force me into the army . . . either way I'm the kind of man he wants me to be. Either way he wins.

GIRL You can go to jail, or leave the country.

YOUNG MAN Is that the only way I can win? How can I do that? I never learned how.

GIRL Why can't you?

YOUNG MAN Because it would be running away . . . and it takes more courage than I've got. I don't know what to do.

GIRL Stay here. In another year you'll be through with school, and maybe the war will be over . . .

YOUNG MAN And maybe it won't. Maybe it'll never be over.

GIRL You can get your parents to change their minds.

YOUNG MAN My father doesn't even consider the School of Music a school. He thinks it's like piano lessons. (*Pause*) It's amazing. All those lessons, and practicing, and winding the Goddamned metronome . . .

GIRL   I played flute until eighth grade.

YOUNG MAN   Is that why you have such strong lips!

GIRL (*Smiles*)   Must be . . .

YOUNG MAN   Whatever I play is for you. I mean it! I think of you . . . and us . . . and no matter what it is, it comes out eight-dimensional.

GIRL   Knowing it's you playing makes it that way for me, too.

YOUNG MAN   You know how I know I love you?

GIRL (*She curls up close to him on the bed*)   Uh-uh. How?

YOUNG MAN   Because when I hug you it's warm.

GIRL   That's it? It's warm no matter who you're hugging.

YOUNG MAN   No it's not. Not inside. It's different with you.

GIRL   Thanks, Fingers.

YOUNG MAN   Where'd that come from?

GIRL   I don't know. I think it's a good name for you.

YOUNG MAN   If you call me Fingers, I'll call you Lips.

GIRL   Just in public, okay?

YOUNG MAN   All right. (*They both start laughing loudly*) Are you thinking? . . .

GIRL   The time in the Student Health Service!

YOUNG MAN   Yes, yes!

GIRL   You chased me through there screaming, "Don't think you can hang a paternity suit on me! I bought you those pills myself!"

YOUNG MAN   Everybody knew we were kidding.

GIRL   They did not! Anyway, it was a riot.

YOUNG MAN   I bet they have people pull that in there twice a day. (*He pauses*) It's so safe here. Just us, all warm. The rain is the music.

GIRL (*Pauses*)   It is like music. You can hear music in everything.

YOUNG MAN   Everything has music in it.
        (*The* GIRL *sits on the bed, the* YOUNG MAN *stands at stage right. She starts to play the tape of the fugue where she had turned it off. The lights fade out on all but her*)

GIRL   Little plastic tapes . . . (*To where the* YOUNG MAN *was standing*) You're immortal on here! Isn't that amazing?
        (*She listens to the tape*)

YOUNG MAN'S VOICE The rain's letting up.

GIRL I remember every word we said when I listen to this.
(*The lights fade out on the* GIRL. *The* SOLDIER *appears.
The* YOUNG MAN *goes over to him. They stand,
watching offstage*)

YOUNG MAN It always smells good after a rain.

SOLDIER The son of a bitch won't talk.

YOUNG MAN Are they going to kill him?
(*He is cold, matter-of-fact, unconcerned*)

SOLDIER Yeah. They'll leave him here for his buddies to take
down.

YOUNG MAN Only one more soldier.

SOLDIER (*Laughs*) All right, let's get going.
(*He slaps the* YOUNG MAN *on the shoulder*)

YOUNG MAN Yeah.
(*The music stops. The lights rise. The* MOTHER *is sitting beneath the tree. She has a checkbook and en-
velopes. She is writing. Her husband enters, carrying
an aluminum ladder in one hand and a rectangular
box in the other*)

FATHER Wait 'til you see what I've got.

MOTHER What'd you get?

FATHER   You're going to love this.
   (*He is setting up the ladder beneath the tree*)

MOTHER   What is it?

FATHER (*Securing the ladder*)   Okay. (*He turns to her; she is writing*) If you're not interested . . .

MOTHER   I am interested! Stop acting like a two-year-old.

FATHER   Look! (*He picks up the box from the ground, puts it on the tray in front of her, and opens it*) A swing!

MOTHER   A swing?

FATHER   It's not velvet, but it's red!
   (*He holds up the red wooden seat*)

MOTHER   Who's going to swing on it?

FATHER   We are!

MOTHER   I'm too old to . . .

FATHER   Too old? If I'm not too old to push you, you're not too old to swing!

MOTHER   You'll hurt your back.

FATHER   I'll be careful. Stop mothering me.

MOTHER   Who's mothering you? Go ahead and hurt yourself.

FATHER It isn't even up yet and you've managed to spoil the whole surprise.

MOTHER If there was somebody to use it . . . if we had children . . .

FATHER We'll use it.

MOTHER I suppose the kids from next door can come over . . . What about my geraniums?

FATHER I'm not going to hang it over the trunk, you know. You can't swing there! It'll be way out on a limb.

MOTHER (*Laughing at his unintended meaning*) That's for sure.

FATHER What's for sure?

MOTHER It'll be way out on a limb! How far can that be? Two feet?

FATHER We're going to hang it right now. So you can supervise. As usual.

MOTHER You shouldn't have carried that big ladder out here by yourself.

FATHER It's aluminum. Hardly weighs a thing. (*He goes to the ladder*) This shouldn't take too long.

MOTHER (*She rises to help her husband, goes to him*) I'll hold the ladder for you.

FATHER (*Starting up the ladder*) How's the checkbook?

MOTHER Fine. Never been better.

FATHER How much do we have in the checkbook?

MOTHER Oh, about seventeen hundred.

FATHER How much are we going to have when you're finished?

MOTHER Fifteen dollars. (*He starts*) I'm only kidding. I don't know yet. Be careful.

FATHER You just hold on down there.

MOTHER I am.

FATHER Yes, yes.

MOTHER This is a hell of a way to break out of middle age.

FATHER It's not as if I'd bought a surfboard. All we're going to do is swing a little.

MOTHER That's us, a couple of swingers.

FATHER (*Reaching to finish tying one rope*) That's one.

MOTHER Who painted it bright red? I like that.

FATHER That's the way it came. I thought you'd like it.

MOTHER   I should do some painting again. It must be three years . . .

FATHER   The last thing you did was the pastel portrait . . .

MOTHER   I know.

FATHER   Whenever I look at it I can see how much you loved him.

MOTHER   I had to force him to sit for it. He was so impatient.

FATHER   All right. I'm coming down.

MOTHER   I'm holding on.
     (*He reaches the ground*)

FATHER (*Looking up*)   Well! We've got a swing! Ready to try it? Here, I'll move the ladder.
     (*He folds it and sets it on the ground. She goes to the swing, pulls the ropes to make sure it is sturdy, and sits down. She swings a little, keeping her feet on the ground in the same place*)

MOTHER   It's like being a little girl again. I guess I'm not too old after all.

FATHER   Hell no!
     (*He gives her a push*)

MOTHER   Not too high . . . I'm worried about that tree branch. (*She laughs, tilts her head back*) It feels so free . . . I wish you didn't have to go away again.

73

FATHER   I don't want to. I have to.

MOTHER   You've said that for twenty-six years.

FATHER   And I've meant it for twenty-six years. But there's nothing else I could do; if I changed now, where I'd make as much money?

MOTHER   Everybody gets hooked in their responsibilities. I don't know why I go on fighting it. (*They swing silently for a moment*) Do you know how old I am?

FATHER   Forty-four.

MOTHER   And you're fifty-one.

FATHER   We both look ten years younger than that!

MOTHER   (*Laughing*)   I agree completely! (*Pause*) I wish I felt it! God, I wish we could have another child.

FATHER   That's all you need . . . having to go through all that again. Could you really do it?

MOTHER   I suppose not. I wish we'd have had more children when we could.

FATHER   Not me. One son was more than enough.

MOTHER   (*She stops swinging*)   What would enough have been? None?

FATHER   I didn't mean it.

MOTHER   Loving one son was all you could handle? It must have been a tremendous exertion for you, raising your only son.

FATHER   I said I didn't mean it.

MOTHER   When were you ever here long enough . . .

FATHER   I was here as much as I could!

MOTHER   And one son was too much for you. Well, you had to have an heir, you know. A prince to inherit the fortune. Who are you going to leave the kingdom to now? A pet dog? A pet charity?

FATHER   Stop baiting me!

MOTHER   I'm not baiting you. You just told me that *no* sons would have been . . . enough for you. No sons, a minimal amount of sex . . .

FATHER   I loved my son . . . I gave him everything he wanted, everything I could. And he turned into a fine man.

MOTHER   He had to die so you could say that.

FATHER   When I look at that portrait you did of him, I see his determination.

MOTHER   I'm sick of hearing you worship him! How much did either of you worship the other when he was alive?

FATHER   He proved himself . . .

MOTHER   Why should he have to prove himself! How can anyone ask another for that kind of proof! He died for something he didn't believe in, he was forced into it.

FATHER   He went because it was his responsibility.

MOTHER   He went because he wasn't strong enough not to! He went because he was trapped!

FATHER (*Pauses*)   I'm going to put this back.
      (*He picks up the ladder*)

MOTHER (*She starts; appears afraid to be alone*)   Are you coming back out?

FATHER   Yes. I'm coming back.
      (*He leaves. The* MOTHER *returns to her chair behind the folding tray. She stares straight ahead. The* YOUNG MAN *comes out, sits cross-legged on the ground*)

YOUNG MAN   Mom? Is this okay?

MOTHER (*Noticing him for the first time*)   Yes, it's fine. Just hold it.
      (*She takes out a sketch pad and a box of pastels*)

YOUNG MAN   What are you going to do with this when it's through?

76

MOTHER (*Sketching him*) We'll put it over the piano.

YOUNG MAN I've been framed! It's all a mistake! I thought you'd give it to Dad for a dartboard.

MOTHER Stop it.

YOUNG MAN I was just kidding. I know you're making a dartboard for yourself.

MOTHER If you don't sit still, I'm going to make a dartboard out of you! (*She sketches silently*) This is the most relaxing thing in the world. I can feel myself loosening up, slowing down . . .

YOUNG MAN You look like you're enjoying it.

MOTHER I am. You should try it some time.

YOUNG MAN I would, except if I picked up your hobby, Dad would probably think I was rejecting him.

MOTHER Don't do your father's thinking for him. He doesn't need any assistance from you.

YOUNG MAN I didn't mean it.

MOTHER You say a lot of things you don't mean. Sit still. And most of it is cruel. When you say something mean about your father, you're saying something mean about me.

YOUNG MAN No I'm not.

77

MOTHER You are, because I love him. If you have any battles to settle with him, don't try and get me on your side, because I won't come.

YOUNG MAN You can sure swing like a pendulum. You can go from the most possessive mother to the most dispassionate observer in one swoop.

MOTHER Don't you think it's time you were . . . dispossessed?

YOUNG MAN Yes, but don't go to extremes.

MOTHER It's funny about possession. How the possessed holds on as strongly as the possessor.

YOUNG MAN Are you almost done?

MOTHER Yes. A couple of more sittings and you'll be through. Then I'll have you to look at every day when you're gone. (*She finishes up*) All right. That's it.

YOUNG MAN You sure?

MOTHER Of course I'm sure. Dismissed!
(*She puts the pad and pastels back*)

YOUNG MAN Okay. See you later.

MOTHER See you later.
(*He exits. She returns to work on the checkbook. The* FATHER *returns*)

FATHER   Baby . . . I'm sorry.

MOTHER   I'm sorry too. It's my own fault. It's been three years and I'm just starting to feel it. I still think that I'm a mother . . .

FATHER   We can't let anything separate us.

MOTHER   I agree. Nothing is as important as holding on to what we have left . . . if we had talked things out as we went along, rather than being afraid to say anything, sitting on our thoughts . . . we're too old for this!

FATHER   I guess we are.

MOTHER   (*Rises, going to swing*)   What I said about your being a father . . . I was blaming you. It's no one's fault.

FATHER   I guess I was wrong more times than I was right. But it's too late to do anything about it now. (MOTHER *sits on the swing. He pushes her slowly, gently*) I wish we had another child. Another beginning. I couldn't bring myself to say that I did, for all this time. But I do.
(*They swing as the lights fade out*)

Curtain

Act Three

ACT THREE

The YOUNG MAN *and* GIRL *sit with their backs against the tree. It is evening. Stars are out.*

YOUNG MAN   I just want to lie here and never move again. I'll grow some roots, and I'll just stay here. The wind can put me to sleep. I'll be safe. Everything quiet and peaceful.

GIRL   I wonder what it would be like to be like that. To be rooted in the same place. To be physically connected to the earth.

YOUNG MAN   You'd be a part of everything. Things would come and go, you'd see everything and know you'd always be there, no matter what.

GIRL   And you'd never have to make choices or decide anything . . . Like part of a cycle.

YOUNG MAN   Round and round we go. Burn up and burn out. The same words and games and irreparable damages . . . and "The earth shall run red with the redundance of blood." . . .

GIRL   What's that?

YOUNG MAN   An Irish folk song. About a guy telling his girl how he'll think of her when he's away fighting:

"But the earth shall run red with the redundance of blood, / And the earth shall rock beneath thy tread, / And flame wrap hill and wood, / And gun peal and slogan cry, wake many a glen serene, / E'er you shall fade, e'er you shall die, my dark Rosaleen, / My own Rosaleen."

GIRL   "My dark Rosaleen."

YOUNG MAN   The gun peals are still the same and the slogans read like billboards. People still tally their lives in wins and losses—a girl, a war, a job . . . it's all the same.

GIRL   "E'er you shall fade, e'er you shall die . . ."

YOUNG MAN   Yes.

GIRL   I knew it would be like this! Bit by bit, the pieces are removed, and there's nothing left.

YOUNG MAN   I'm not going away forever. We'll write . . .

GIRL   What a desparate way to hold onto people.

YOUNG MAN   Well, if you think I'm going to call you from half way around the world . . .

GIRL   Just come back.

YOUNG MAN   Yes, dear. Look, I'm going to be a very good little follower. I'll stay inconspicuously near the end of the line. I won't go into anything first, or go anywhere by myself, and nothing will happen.

GIRL   And you won't kill anyone.

YOUNG MAN   Hell, no.

GIRL   All right. (*She pauses*) I'll wait for you. You know that.

YOUNG MAN   Two years is a long time. Are you going to go out?

GIRL   If somebody asks me . . .

YOUNG MAN   You are?

GIRL   Well, I'm not going to be an old maid and sit in for two years. Besides—you'll go out too. You'll probably spend all your weekends in brothels.

YOUNG MAN   And where would I get the money?

GIRL   I'll send it to you.

YOUNG MAN   All right. I'll do it for you.

GIRL   Stop it!

YOUNG MAN   See? See how things fall apart? They don't do it by themselves, you know.

GIRL   I don't let them.

YOUNG MAN   Sure you do.

GIRL Why? Because I said I want to go out? I'm just being realistic. Two years . . .

YOUNG MAN If I can wait two years, you can.

GIRL If somebody calls up and asks me if I want to go to a movie or something, I'm going to go. I don't want to think I would have to hide it from you.

YOUNG MAN You don't have to hide it. I just don't like it. Did you think I would?

GIRL It's not like I'm going to be sleeping with them . . .

YOUNG MAN It leads to that! Look what happened to us.

GIRL You're the most possessive, jealous . . .

YOUNG MAN You're damned right I am.

GIRL You have no reason to be. You're not going to lose me. (*She pauses*) Well?

YOUNG MAN I don't want to forget how that sounded. I'm playing it over in my mind.

GIRL I mean it. Everything there is . . . is us. I mean it.

YOUNG MAN Okay. Want to count stars?

GIRL Let's just sit here and be quiet. It'll make the time seem longer.

86

YOUNG MAN   You know what would be nice?

GIRL   What?

YOUNG MAN   If we could live on a farm.

GIRL   That would be nice.

YOUNG MAN   We'd be alone, and have grass and trees all around . . .

GIRL   And all this space for the kids to play . . . if you're very successful they can each have their own horse.

YOUNG MAN   And if I'm not, they can each have their own chicken.

GIRL   They wouldn't like that.

YOUNG MAN   We could go for walks and have picnics.

GIRL *(She rises)*   Every night you could give us a concert . . .

YOUNG MAN   The chickens, too.

GIRL   We'd be the best audience you ever had.
(*She sits stage right, where she remains in a dim light*)

YOUNG MAN   Everything would be just like we planned. Everything planned out. Everything.
(*The* MOTHER *appears at stage left*)

MOTHER I remember when you were a Boy Scout, your troop went on an overnight hike to Burnet Woods. We got you a knapsack and a mess kit and a canteen . . . you looked like you were going to hike cross-country.

YOUNG MAN All I remember is that it rained and you drove over in the middle of the night to make me come home.

MOTHER It didn't help much. You were sick for a week.

YOUNG MAN The embarrassment was the worst of it.

MOTHER Could it have been worth getting pneumonia to stay?

YOUNG MAN Well, not now. I don't think so. But then it was a big deal. I felt like such a baby.

MOTHER I think you turned out all right in spite of it all.

YOUNG MAN I remember all that so clearly. How come those thoughts stick out in your mind and you can even feel like you felt back then? I can feel the woods and the rain . . . I can even smell them.

MOTHER I . . . I don't suppose I'll get another chance to be alone with you before you go.

YOUNG MAN I guess not. Any last words?

MOTHER I don't have to tell you anything. You know it all backwards and forwards already.

88

Priscilla Pointer as the MOTHER and
David Birney as the YOUNG MAN.

YOUNG MAN   I guess I do.

MOTHER (*She smiles*)   You're not a baby any more!

YOUNG MAN (*He laughs*)   You noticed.

MOTHER   When you come back, you should be quite a man. Even your father will have to watch how he addresses you!

YOUNG MAN   I don't think I'll ever be too big for Dad. I can't imagine ever being big enough to handle him.

MOTHER   He's going to miss you.

YOUNG MAN   Is he?

MOTHER   Yes, he is.

YOUNG MAN   I've always missed him.

MOTHER   Tell him that you're going to miss him. It would make him feel good to know.

YOUNG MAN   Yes. I'm going to. I will miss him.

MOTHER   Will you write as often as you can?

YOUNG MAN   Yes.

MOTHER   It's important. It's not like you were a couple of hours away at school.

YOUNG MAN   I will.

MOTHER   Just write . . . as much as you can.

YOUNG MAN   You have my tapes someplace safe?

MOTHER   They're in the chest of drawers.

YOUNG MAN   I wanted to make some more, but I just didn't get around to it.

MOTHER   When you get back you can make up some new ones. That's something to look forward to.

YOUNG MAN   You going to plant the geraniums again this year?

MOTHER   Yes. Don't I always?

YOUNG MAN   I guess that's why I like them. They're a part of the house. I can't remember one year that we've lived here that you haven't planted them.

MOTHER   They're a national institution!

YOUNG MAN   Almost.

MOTHER   It's a warm night. The stars are out.
      (*They are silent*)

YOUNG MAN   When I get back, do you think we could go on a trip? Maybe up to Canada. We've never been there. I could help with the driving.

MOTHER   I think we should plan on it! Something to look forward to.

YOUNG MAN   Do you think Dad'll want to?

MOTHER   Why wouldn't he?

YOUNG MAN   We haven't gone on a vacation in a long time.

MOTHER   We were thinking that we might go to Europe next spring . . . it's been six years since we were there.

YOUNG MAN   You should—I won't be costing you anything, so you can sort of shift the funds a little.

MOTHER   We'll see.

YOUNG MAN   We'll be scattered all over the world!

MOTHER   A real bunch of gypsies.

YOUNG MAN   Send me a postcard . . .

MOTHER   You know we will . . . we're not even gone yet and you're worried that we won't write.

YOUNG MAN   I'm not.

MOTHER   I'm just teasing.
    (*She laughs*)

YOUNG MAN   And listen, I don't want any teary good-byes. If you cry, I'm going to cry, and I don't want to do that.

MOTHER   I don't cry!

YOUNG MAN   Just don't.

MOTHER   My word of honor. A fast handshake and that's it.

YOUNG MAN   You don't have to go to the other extreme. I want to kiss you good-bye. Just don't cry.

MOTHER   I won't!

YOUNG MAN   Okay. (*The* MOTHER *sits stage left in a dim light*) I can hardly remember your ever crying. There was one time . . . it was a gray, boring Saturday afternoon. It was cold and getting ready to rain. I looked into the living room and you were sitting on that little chair by the front window, looking straight ahead and not making any noise. I wondered why you were crying. You said you just felt like it. (*He pauses*) I wish you didn't have to be here by yourself. A big house and nobody to live in it. (*He looks around*) Not much time left, not even a day. Not even twelve hours. It's almost over. (*His* FATHER *appears*) Hi, Dad.

FATHER   How are you, buddy?

YOUNG MAN   Nervous.

FATHER   Well, don't worry. Think of all the people who've been through it. Be a man.

YOUNG MAN   I'm trying.

FATHER   I know you are. We'll be with you every minute, you know that.

YOUNG MAN   Yes.

FATHER   Have you thought about what you want to do when you get back?

YOUNG MAN   I'm still thinking about what I'm going to be doing when I'm gone.

FATHER   You'll have plenty of time to decide.

YOUNG MAN   I suppose I'll pick things up where I left off.

FATHER   If you want to go back to school . . . I mean full time.

YOUNG MAN   I'd like to very much. I couldn't afford full time without a scholarship . . .

FATHER   (*Pauses*)   I was thinking I could give you some money . . .

YOUNG MAN   I don't want you to give me anything. Isn't it a little late to change your mind?

FATHER   I'm not changing my mind. I never wanted you to leave school. I'm just trying to make it easier for you. What do you say about my making you a loan . . .

YOUNG MAN   And the conditions?

FATHER   No conditions! Just go back to school. You can enroll in the School of Music. If that's what you want.

YOUNG MAN   You wait until the last night before I leave.

FATHER   Well, isn't it what you want?

YOUNG MAN   Yes, yes, it's what I want. But the last minute! . . . Why do you think I left school? I had to stand up to you and say, This is what I want, this is what I think is honest and right for me.

FATHER   You quit because you didn't want to face your responsibilities. You thought you were cornered, so rather than make things better, you ran away. Just like you ran away from summer camp.

YOUNG MAN   I thought what I did was pretty brave.

FATHER   It was stupid. Look what's happened. Don't you think I'd rather you were in school than going off?

YOUNG MAN   Don't you think I wish I were too? And now this. You. What a joke it's turned into.

FATHER   It's not a joke.

YOUNG MAN   Of course it is. None of this even had to happen.

FATHER   You'll be back. You can pick up where you left off.

YOUNG MAN   What an amazing thing this is! I have to think it over a few times and make sure I have it all straight. I don't want to get any of it mixed up.

FATHER   Everything'll be all right.

YOUNG MAN   Sure it will. Just don't change your mind again. You know how important the money is. I've got to have it! Promise you won't change your mind.

FATHER   A deal's a deal. (*He pauses*) Did you see your mother?

YOUNG MAN   Yes. She was just out here. We talked.

FATHER   She's going to miss you. More than I will, I think.

YOUNG MAN   Why more than you?

FATHER   I mean, because you and she have been together more . . .

YOUNG MAN We didn't want it that way. Not that we minded too much. But we'd rather have been with you.

FATHER (*He pauses*) I didn't think so.

YOUNG MAN We would have, but saying it now does you as much good as your loan does me. (*He pauses*) It's not so funny after all.

FATHER It's not funny.

YOUNG MAN I love you, Dad. I hate you enough to kill you sometimes, but I love you.

FATHER I love you too, buddy.

YOUNG MAN (*Smiling*) My old man.

FATHER Yeah, he's getting there. They'll have to put him out to pasture soon.

YOUNG MAN You're not old! You're hardly fat and . . . hardly bald.

FATHER That makes me feel a hell of a lot better. (*He pauses*) You going to make me proud of you?

YOUNG MAN Yes, I am. I want you to be proud of me.

FATHER Everything's going to be all right. I am proud of you. You're a good boy.

YOUNG MAN   I wish you'd tell me that more often.

FATHER   Yeah, you'd go around more conceited than you already are . . .

YOUNG MAN   I'm not conceited!

FATHER   Oh, sure.

YOUNG MAN   I'm just extremely talented, charming, handsome . . .

FATHER   And you have about as much common sense as a stick of wood.

YOUNG MAN   I'll get some! Somewhere. I'm not very old, you know.

FATHER   You're old enough to start planning ahead, using a little sense.

YOUNG MAN   I'll come through it all fine. I know you'll be surprised, but I will.

FATHER   I know you will. Let's go see Mom.

YOUNG MAN   I'll be in in a minute. I want to tell the backyard good-bye.

FATHER   Is there anything you're not going to miss?

YOUNG MAN   Not if I can help it. I want to remember everything.

FATHER Come in soon. (*He stands upstage left in a pool of light*) You don't want to sit out here by yourself.

YOUNG MAN It's getting cold. I remember when you had to go away on a trip, you'd get up around five. I used to set my clock so I could get up and tell you good-bye. You used to get angry because you thought I needed my sleep more than telling you good-bye. I thought it was the other way around. No common sense. We never could agree on anything.

GIRL Are you getting cold?

YOUNG MAN Yes, I'm cold.

MOTHER Why don't you come inside? It's late.

YOUNG MAN I have to remember everything. (*The* LITTLE BOY *appears. He carries a very real-looking toy rifle. But it is still noticeably a toy*) Nothing sinks in with you. Let's see it.
        (*He puts out his hand and the* LITTLE BOY *gives him the rifle. He puts it down next to him*)

LITTLE BOY Weren't you going to tell me good-bye?

YOUNG MAN No. Why should I tell you good-bye?

LITTLE BOY I thought we were friends.

YOUNG MAN Yes. I was going to tell you good-bye.

LITTLE BOY   Will you write me a letter when you get there?

YOUNG MAN   If I have time. Do you collect stamps or something?

LITTLE BOY   No. I want the letter.

YOUNG MAN   You really want to hear from me? All right.

LITTLE BOY   I have a pen pal in Ireland.

YOUNG MAN   That's nice. Where'd you get the gun?

LITTLE BOY   A present. It looks real, doesn't it?

YOUNG MAN   Yes. Like the real thing. Have you used it much?

LITTLE BOY   Just a few times.

YOUNG MAN   Show me how to work it. I might as well do a little planning ahead.
    (*He looks toward his* FATHER)

LITTLE BOY (*Picking up the gun*)   You just hold it and look through here and pull this back . . . and when you spot your target, you pull the trigger.

YOUNG MAN   Simple enough.

LITTLE BOY   Didn't you have a rifle?

99

YOUNG MAN   Only six-shooters, partner. Now that's a man's gun! What kind of ammo does this take?

LITTLE BOY   Caps.

YOUNG MAN   The big stuff, huh? See that jungle cat? Watch me bag him. (*Turning quickly and firing*) Bang! Right in the left eye. Didn't touch the skin. Did you ever play firing squad?

LITTLE BOY   No. How do you play?

YOUNG MAN   You haven't lived until you play firing squad, kid. Okay. Stand over there. Ten paces.
(*The* LITTLE BOY *backs off ten paces*)

YOUNG MAN   That's fine. Any last words? No? Ready, aim, fire. Bang. You're dead, kid. Fall to the ground.

LITTLE BOY (*He laughs*)   Just like that?

YOUNG MAN   I said fall to the ground. (*The* LITTLE BOY *follows the instructions*) That's very good. An authentic execution.

LITTLE BOY   Is that all there is?

YOUNG MAN   Oh no. That's only half of it. Here, take your gun. Here! (*The* LITTLE BOY *comes, takes the gun*) Now go back where you were. (*The* LITTLE BOY *backs off to where he was before*) Point the gun at me.

LITTLE BOY   I don't want to.

YOUNG MAN   I'm the commanding officer here. Do what I say and shut up! Point it at me. (*The* LITTLE BOY *does not answer*) Yes, sir.

LITTLE BOY   Yes, sir.

YOUNG MAN   Ready, aim, fire. Did you pull the trigger?

LITTLE BOY   Not yet.

YOUNG MAN   Then pull it! And shout bang!

LITTLE BOY   Yes, sir. (*He pulls the trigger*) Bang!
(*The* YOUNG MAN *lets out a loud cry, staring directly at the* LITTLE BOY. *The* LITTLE BOY *drops his rifle*)

YOUNG MAN   Well?

LITTLE BOY   You scared me.

YOUNG MAN   Just a passing cry in the night. Really nothing. This is good practice, don't you think?

LITTLE BOY   Practice?

YOUNG MAN   Well, you can't expect to step right into a firing squad—at either end of the gun—and know what to do without some practice, can you?

LITTLE BOY   This isn't a very good game.

YOUNG MAN   Game? Who said anything about a game? We're learning to fire a real gun. For real. At real people. What kind of soldier are you, talking about games? Men's lives are at stake, boy. Every mother's son must do his duty. That includes you. Everybody pulls their own around here. (*The* LITTLE BOY *puts the gun down next to the* YOUNG MAN) What are you doing?

LITTLE BOY   What?

YOUNG MAN   The rifle! What are you doing?

LITTLE BOY   I put it down next to you.

YOUNG MAN   I know you put it down next to me. A soldier never puts his gun down. Pick it up! Yes, sir!

LITTLE BOY   Yes, sir.

BOY   A soldier dies with his boots on and his rifle in his hands.

LITTLE BOY   I think I'd better go.

YOUNG MAN   Go? Where are you going? Don't go. Listen, we were only playing. Hey! Do you think I'll be a good soldier? Did I sound rough and tough and brave?

LITTLE BOY   I guess so.

YOUNG MAN   Well, did I? You can tell. You heard.

LITTLE BOY   Yes.

YOUNG MAN   I thought so too.

LITTLE BOY   Are you scared about going?

YOUNG MAN   Scared? Why should I be scared? All I'm doing is the common, expected thing. If it's so common and expected, it couldn't take much to do it, could it? Now if I had to do something like go to jail . . . then I might be scared.

LITTLE BOY   I'd be scared either way.

YOUNG MAN   You miss the whole point. All I'm doing is following orders. That's my duty. So why should I have to worry about feeling scared? Or feeling anything?

LITTLE BOY   I don't know what you—

YOUNG MAN   Come on! It's a simple matter of courage and integrity, following one's star, and marching to a different drummer. Things like that. Then there's a bit of the Lord's Prayer, the Golden Rule, and "Let your conscience be your guide." That's Jiminy Cricket, you know. Ever see *Pinocchio?*

LITTLE BOY   Yes.

YOUNG MAN   Good film, huh?

LITTLE BOY   Yes.

YOUNG MAN   I saw it when I was about nine. It scared the hell out of me. That mean wolf, and that horrible carnival . . . and that whole thing with being a puppet. Isn't that funny? A puppet turning into a boy, and his nose growing whenever he lied? (*He pauses*) You know . . . I didn't . . . tell you the truth.

LITTLE BOY   About what?

YOUNG MAN   About being scared. I am. Very.

LITTLE BOY   That's all right.

YOUNG MAN   Are you still going to write me? (*He pauses*) I'll write and tell you all about it.

LITTLE BOY   I hope you do all right.

YOUNG MAN   Don't you want your gun?
            (*He picks it up and points it at him*)

LITTLE BOY   No, I don't want it.

YOUNG MAN   Come on, take your rifle. You know you want it. Don't say you don't just to please me.

LITTLE BOY   I don't want it. Just leave it there.

YOUNG MAN   Well, why don't you want it?

LITTLE BOY   I don't want it! I said I don't want it!

YOUNG MAN (*He puts the rifle down*)   I'm sorry. I'll see you.
(*The* SOLDIER *enters upstage right and poses at ease,
in a pool of light. The* FATHER *is opposite him, posed
upstage left in a light*)

LITTLE BOY   Yeah, I'll see you.
(*He sits downstage center on the floor*)

YOUNG MAN (*He pauses*)   It's hot out here, just sitting and
waiting. Shirt's sticking to my back. I hate it like this, wiping sweat out of my eyes. Damn. (*He wipes his forehead
with the back of his hand*) I'll just lie here and let the
breeze dry my face. Ah. That feels good. Just close my
eyes and put my head back. (*He leans back against the
tree*) I have to remember all these things . . . find them
. . . make sure I have them. Remember everything.

FATHER   Come on in now.

YOUNG MAN   I have to remember what everyone looks like.
It's hard to do that. I wonder how people can draw people
from memory . . . I have in mind . . . a family portrait.
Everyone posed together. (*He pauses*) God, my stomach
hurts. I wonder why my life isn't flashing before my eyes.
Am I going to have to recall every damn thing myself?

GIRL   I don't want to remember.

MOTHER   Why don't you come in now?

YOUNG MAN My horizons are not unlimited. I can't see a damned thing. See how brave I was? Didn't you think I behaved like a real man? I wish I had my giraffe with me. (*He laughs*) Hey, you're tickling me . . . ow! That hurts! What's this? I can't feel my hands. (*He pauses*) No twelve babies. No babies. (*He cries*) Mom! Dad! Please!

(*The lights fade to black*)

Curtain

ABOUT THE AUTHOR

RON COWEN is twenty-two years old; he received a B.A. in English in 1966 from U.C.L.A. and is currently finishing a master's thesis for the Annenberg Center for Communication Arts and Science of the University of Pennsylvania. *Summertree* is his first full-length play and was given a performance during the O'Neill Foundation Conference for Playwrights at Waterford, Connecticut, last summer. Mr. Cowen is working on a television play commissioned by the C.B.S. Playhouse for telecast in the fall. This year he was elected to the New Dramatists Committee and holds the distinction of being the youngest member in that organization's history. Mr. Cowen was the recipient of a 1967-68 Drama Desk-Vernon Rice Award.